RELATIONSHIPS

101

RELATIONSHIPS

101

WHAT EVERY LEADER NEEDS TO KNOW

JOHN C. MAXWELL

THOMAS NELSON PUBLISHERS®
Nashville

A Division of Thomas Nelson, Inc.
www.ThomasNelson.com

Published in Nashville, Tennessee, by Thomas Nelson, Inc.

Scripture quotations noted NIV are from the HOLY BIBLE: NEW
INTERNATIONAL VERSION®. Copyright 1973, 1978, 1984 by
International Bible Society. Used by permission of Zondervan
Publishing House. All rights reserved.

Portions of this book were previously published in *Becoming a Person of
Influence, The 17 Essential Qualities of a Team Player, The 21 Irrefutable
Laws of Leadership, The 21 Indispensable Qualities of a Leader*,
and *Your Road Map for Success.*

Library of Congress Cataloging-in-Publication Data

Maxwell, John C., 1947–
Relationships 101 : what every leader needs to know / John C. Maxwell.
p. cm.
"Portions of this book were previously published in *Becoming a person of
influence, The 17 essential qualities of a team player, The 21
irrefutable laws of leadership, The 21 indispensable qualities of a
leader*, and *Your road map for success.*"
ISBN 0-7852-6351-9 (hardcover)
1. Leadership. 2. Interpersonal relations. 3. Success in business.
I. Title.
HD57.7 .M39427
658.4'092—dc22
2003021381

Printed in the United States of America

05 06 07 08 09 WOZ 11 10 9 8 7

CONTENTS

PUBLISHER'S PREFACE

No one undertakes a journey alone. We depend upon others constantly—in ways both tangible and intangible—to move us toward our destination. We cannot succeed without the help of others, but forming positive relationships can be a challenge. In *Relationships 101,* John Maxwell reveals the secrets behind connecting with other people. He points out the barriers to relationships, emphasizes the shared needs among people, and describes the ways to connect with others on many different levels. Naturally, he also shows how relationships impact leadership. Most of all, he explains how relationships help us reach our fullest potential.

As America's leadership expert, Dr. Maxwell has spent a lifetime helping others become successful. Through this series of books, his goal is to help others become a REAL success in four crucial areas: Relationships, Equipping, Attitude, and Leadership. *Relationships 101* provides the fundamentals you need to master relationship skills. *Equipping 101, Attitude*

101, and *Leadership 101* will give you the other skills you need to reach your goals.

We are delighted to publish *Relationships 101* because we recognize the significance of positive relationships in every aspect of life. Building positive relationships with others involves risk, but Dr. Maxwell shows that the rewards outweigh that risk. This short course on relationships will equip you with valuable skills for connecting with others as you journey toward success.

PART I

THE NATURE
OF RELATIONSHIPS

I

WHY ARE RELATIONSHIPS
IMPORTANT TO SUCCESS?

Relationships are the glue that holds team members together.

I n the early 1960s, Michael Deaver was a young man with
a political bent looking for a leader he could believe in
and follow. The person he found was an actor-turned-
politician named Ronald Reagan. In 1966, Reagan was
elected governor of California, an office he would hold for
two terms, from 1967 to 1975. During that tenure, Deaver
became Reagan's deputy chief of staff, an office he also held
when Reagan became the nation's fortieth president.

Deaver admired many things about the man he worked
with for thirty years: his convictions and love of country, his
understanding of himself, his skill as a communicator, and his
honesty. Deaver said, "I would go so far as to say that he was
actually incapable of dishonesty."[1] But perhaps what was most
impressive about Ronald Reagan was his ability to relate to
people.

Deaver commented, "Ronald Reagan was one of the shyest

men I'd ever met."[2] Yet the president was able to connect with anyone, whether a head of state, a blue-collar worker, or a feisty member of the press. When asked about why Reagan had such rapport with the press corps, Deaver remarked, "Well, Reagan basically liked people, whether they were part of the press corps or whether they were just ordinary people. That comes through. While many of the press wouldn't agree with Reagan's policy, they genuinely liked him as a person."[3]

Part of Reagan's skill came from his natural charisma and glib verbal aptitude developed in Hollywood. But even greater was his ability to relate to people, something he honed while traveling the country for a decade as the spokesman for General Electric.

It's said that Reagan could make anyone feel like his best friend, even someone he'd never met before. But more important, he connected with the people closest to him. He truly cared about the people on his team. "The chief of staff, or the gardener, or a secretary would all be treated the same, as far as he was concerned," remembered Deaver. "They were all important."[4]

Deaver related a story that tells much about the connection the two men experienced. In 1975, Reagan gave a speech to a group of conservation-minded hunters in San Francisco, and the organization gave him a small bronze lion as a gift. At the time, Deaver admired it and told Governor Reagan how beautiful he thought it was.

Ten years later, Deaver prepared to bring his service to President Reagan to an end after having written his letter of resignation. Reagan asked Deaver to come to the Oval Office the next morning. As the deputy chief of staff entered the room, the president stood in front of his desk to greet him.

"Mike," he said, "all night I've been trying to think of something to give you that would be a reminder of all the great times we had together." Then Reagan turned around and picked up something from his desk. "You kinda liked this little thing, as I recall," the president said, his eyes moist. And he handed the bronze lion to Deaver, who was totally over-come. He couldn't believe that Reagan had remembered that about him all those years. That lion has held a place of honor in Deaver's home ever since.

SOLID RELATIONSHIPS

Everyone liked being around Ronald Reagan because he loved people and connected with them. He understood that relationships were the glue that held his team members together—the more solid the relationships, the more cohesive his team.

Just about everything you do depends on teamwork. It

doesn't matter whether you are a leader or follower, coach or player, teacher or student, parent or child, CEO or nonprofit worker; you will be involved with other people. The question is, will your involvement with others be successful? Your best chance for leadership also depends upon connecting with those on your team. Here is how you know whether you have built solid relationships with others. Look for the following five characteristics in your relationships:

1. RESPECT

When it comes to relationships, everything begins with respect, with the desire to place value on other people. Human relations author Les Giblin said, "You can't make the other fellow feel important in your presence if you secretly feel that he is a nobody."

The thing about respect is that you should show it to others, even before they have done anything to warrant it, simply because they are human beings. But at the same time, you should always expect to have to earn it from others. And the place you earn it the quickest is on difficult ground.

2. SHARED EXPERIENCES

Respect can lay the foundation for a good relationship, but it alone is not enough. You can't be relational with someone you don't know. It requires shared experiences over time. And that's not always easy to achieve. For example, right after Brian Billick, coach of the Baltimore Ravens, won the 2001 Super Bowl, he was asked about the team's chances for repeating a championship season. He commented that it would be very difficult. Why? Because 25 to 30 percent of the team changes every year. Newer players don't have the shared experiences with the team that are needed to succeed.

3. TRUST

When you respect people and you spend enough time with them to develop shared experiences, you are in a position to develop trust. Trust is essential to all good relationships. Scottish poet George MacDonald observed, "To be trusted is a greater compliment than to be loved." Without trust, you cannot sustain any kind of relationship.

4. RECIPROCITY

One-sided personal relationships don't last. If one person is always the giver and the other is always the receiver, then the relationship will eventually disintegrate. The same is true of all relationships, including those on a team. For people to improve relationally, there has to be give-and-take so that everyone benefits as well as gives. Remember to ask your teammates, colleagues, and friends questions about their hopes, desires, and goals. Give people your full attention. Show others you care about them.

> WHEN IT COMES TO RELATIONSHIPS, EVERYTHING
> BEGINS WITH RESPECT, WITH THE DESIRE TO PLACE
> VALUE ON OTHER PEOPLE.

5. MUTUAL ENJOYMENT

When relationships grow and start to get solid, the people involved begin to enjoy each other. Just being together can turn even unpleasant tasks into positive experiences.

How are you doing when it comes to being relational? Do you spend a lot of time and energy building solid relationships, or are you so focused on results that you tend to overlook (or overrun) others? If the latter is true of you, think about the wise words of George Kienzle and Edward Dare in *Climbing the Executive Ladder:* "Few things will pay you bigger dividends than the time and trouble you take to understand people. Almost nothing will add more to your stature as an executive and a person. Nothing will give you greater satisfaction or bring you more happiness." Becoming a highly relational person brings individual and team success.

2

What Do I Need to Know About Others?

People don't care how much you know,
until they know how much you care.

If your desire is to be successful and to make a positive impact on your world, you need the ability to understand others. Understanding others gives you the potential to influence every area of life, not just the business arena. For example, look at how understanding people helped this mother of a preschooler. She said:

Leaving my four-year-old son in the house, I ran out to throw something in the trash. When I tried to open the door to get back inside, it was locked. I knew that insisting that my son open the door would have resulted in an hour-long battle of the wills. So in a sad voice, I said, "Oh, too bad. You just locked yourself in the house." The door opened at once.

Understanding people certainly impacts your ability to communicate with others. David Burns, a medical doctor and professor of psychiatry at the University of Pennsylvania, observed, "The biggest mistake you can make in trying to talk convincingly is to put your highest priority on expressing your ideas and feelings. What most people really want is to be listened to, respected, and understood. The moment people see that they are being understood, they become more motivated to understand your point of view." If you can learn to understand people—how they think, what they feel, what inspires them, how they're likely to act and react in a given situation—then you can motivate and influence them in a positive way.

WHY PEOPLE FAIL TO UNDERSTAND OTHERS

Lack of understanding concerning others is a recurrent source of tension in our society. I once heard an attorney say, "Half of all the controversies and conflicts that arise among people are caused not by differences of opinion or an inability to agree, but by the lack of understanding of one another." If we could reduce the number of misunderstandings, the courts wouldn't be as crowded, there would be fewer violent crimes, the divorce rate would go down, and the amount of everyday stress most people experience would drop dramatically.

If understanding is such an asset, why don't more people practice it? There are many reasons:

FEAR

Seventeenth-century American colonist William Penn advised, "Neither despise or oppose what thou dost not understand," yet many people seem to do exactly the opposite. When they don't understand others, they often react by becoming fearful. And once they start fearing others, they rarely try to overcome their fear in order to learn more about them. It becomes a vicious cycle.

Unfortunately, fear is evident in the workplace when it comes to employees' reactions toward their leaders. Yet in a healthy work environment, if you give others the benefit of the doubt and replace fear with understanding, everyone can work together positively. All people have to do is follow the advice of President Harry Truman, who said, "When we understand the other fellow's viewpoint—understand what he is trying to do—nine times out of ten he is trying to do right."

SELF-CENTEREDNESS

When fear isn't a stumbling block, self-centeredness often is. People are not self-centered on purpose; it's just in the nature of humans to think of their own interests first. If you want to see an example of that, play with a two-year-old child. He naturally chooses the best toys for himself and insists on his own way.

One way to overcome our natural self-centeredness is to try to see things from other people's perspectives. Talking to a group of salespeople, Art Mortell, author of *World Class Selling*, shared this experience: "Whenever I'm losing at chess, I consistently get up and stand behind my opponent and see the board from his side. Then I discover the stupid moves I've made because I can see it from his viewpoint. The salesperson's challenge is to see the world from the prospect's viewpoint."[1]

That's the challenge for every one of us, no matter what our profession. The following quote reminds us of what our priorities should be when dealing with other people:

A SHORT COURSE IN HUMAN RELATIONS

The least important word: I
The most important word: We
The two most important words: Thank you.
The three most important words: All is forgiven.
The four most important words: What is your opinion?
The five most important words: You did a good job.
The six most important words: I want to understand you
    better.

Failure to Appreciate Differences

The next logical step after leaving behind self-centeredness is learning to recognize and respect everyone else's unique qualities. Instead of trying to cast others in your image, learn to appreciate their differences. If someone has a talent that you don't have, great. The two of you can strengthen each other's weaknesses. If others come from a different culture, broaden your horizons and learn what you can from them. Your new knowledge will help you relate not only to them, but also to others.

Once you learn to appreciate other people's differences, you come to realize that there are many responses to leadership and motivation. Joseph Beck, onetime president of the Kenley Corporation, recognized that truth when he said that "different people are motivated in different ways. A good basketball coach, for example, knows when a player needs a 'kick in the pants.' The main difference is that all players need encouragement and only some need a 'kick in the pants.'"

Failure to Acknowledge Similarities

We all have emotional reactions to what's happening around us. To foster understanding, think of what your emotions would be if you were in the same position as the person you're interacting with. You know what you would want to happen in a given situation. Chances are that the person you're working with has many of the same feelings.

IF YOU TREAT EVERY PERSON YOU MEET AS IF HE OR SHE WERE THE MOST IMPORTANT PERSON IN THE WORLD, YOU'LL COMMUNICATE THAT HE OR SHE *IS* SOMEBODY—TO YOU.

THINGS EVERYBODY NEEDS TO UNDERSTAND ABOUT PEOPLE

Knowing what people need and want is the key to understanding them. And if you can understand them, you can influence them and impact their lives in a positive way. What I know about understanding people can be summed up in the following list:

1. EVERYBODY WANTS TO BE SOMEBODY

There isn't a person in the world who doesn't have the desire to be someone, to have significance. Even the least ambitious and unassuming person wants to be regarded highly by others.

I remember the first time these feelings were stirred strongly within me. It was back when I was in the fourth grade and went to my first basketball game. I stood with my buddies in the balcony of the gym. The thing that I remember most wasn't the game; it was the announcement of the starting lineups. They turned all the lights out, and then some spotlights came on. The announcer called out the names of the starters, and they ran out to the middle of the floor one by one with everybody in the place cheering.

I hung over the balcony that day as a fourth-grade kid and said, "Wow, I'd like that to happen to me." In fact, by the time the introductions were over, I looked at my friend Bobby Wilson, and I said, "Bobby, when I get to high school, they're going to announce my name, and I'm going to run out in the spotlight to the middle of that basketball floor. And the people are going to cheer for me because I'm going to be somebody."

I went home that night and told my dad, "I want to be a basketball player." Soon afterward, he got me a Spalding basketball, and we put a goal on the garage. I used to shovel snow off that driveway to practice my foul shots and play basketball because I had a dream of becoming somebody.

It's funny how that kind of dream can impact your life. In the sixth grade, I played intramural basketball. Our team won a couple of games, so we got to go to the Old Mill Street Gym in Circleville, Ohio, where I'd seen that basketball game in the fourth grade. When we got there, instead of going out onto the floor with the rest of the players as they were warming up, I went to the bench where those high school players had been two years before. I sat right where they had, and I closed my eyes (the equivalent of turning the lights out in the gym). Then in my head I heard my name announced, and I ran out in the middle of the floor.

It felt so good to hear the imaginary applause that I thought, *I'll do it again!* So I did. In fact, I did it three times, and all of a sudden, I realized that my buddies weren't playing basketball; they were just watching me in disbelief. But I didn't care because I was one step closer to being the person I'd dreamed about becoming.

Everybody wants to be regarded and valued by others. In other words, everybody wants to be somebody. Once that piece of information becomes a part of your everyday thinking, you'll gain incredible insight into why people do the things they do. And if you treat every person you meet as if he or she were the most important person in the world, you'll communicate that he or she *is* somebody—to you.

2. Nobody Cares How Much You Know Until He Knows How Much You Care

The moment that people know that you care about them, the way they feel about you changes. Showing others that you care isn't always easy. Your greatest times and fondest memories will come because of people, but so will your most difficult, hurting, and tragic times. People are your greatest assets and your greatest liabilities. The challenge is to keep caring about them no matter what.

I came across an insightful quote called "Paradoxical Commandments of Leadership." Here's what it says:

People are illogical, unreasonable, and self-centered—love them anyway.

If you do good, people will accuse you of selfish ulterior motives—do good anyway.

If you're successful, you'll win false friends and true enemies—succeed anyway.

The good you do today will perhaps be forgotten tomorrow—do good anyway.

Honesty and frankness make you vulnerable—be honest and frank anyway.

The biggest man with the biggest ideas can be shot down by the smallest man with the smallest mind—think big anyway.

People favor underdogs but follow only hot dogs—fight for a few underdogs anyway.

What you spend years building may be destroyed overnight—build anyway.

People really need help but may attack you if you help them—help them anyway.

Give the world the best that you have and you will get

kicked in the teeth—give the world the best that you have anyway.

If better is possible, then good is not enough.

That's the right way to treat people. Besides, you never know which people in your sphere of influence are going to rise up and make a difference in your life and the lives of others.

3. EVERYBODY NEEDS SOMEBODY

Contrary to popular belief, there are no such things as self-made men and women. Everybody needs friendship, encouragement, and help. What people can accomplish by themselves is almost nothing compared to their potential when working with others. And doing things with other people tends to bring contentment. Besides, Lone Rangers are rarely happy people. King Solomon of ancient Israel stated the value of working together this way:

Two are better than one,
     because they have a good return for their work:
If one falls down,
     his friend can help him up.
But pity the man who falls
     and has no one to help him up!

Also, if two lie down together, they will keep warm.
　　But how can one keep warm alone?
Though one may be overpowered,
　　two can defend themselves.
A cord of three strands is not quickly broken.[2]

Everybody needs somebody to come alongside and help. If you understand that, are willing to give to others and help them, and maintain the right motives, their lives and yours can change.

4. EVERYBODY CAN BE SOMEBODY WHEN SOMEBODY UNDERSTANDS AND BELIEVES HER

Once you understand people and believe in them, they really can become somebody. And it doesn't take much effort to help other people feel important. Little things, done deliberately at the right time, can make a big difference.

When was the last time you went out of your way to make people feel special, as if they were somebody? The investment required on your part is totally overshadowed by the impact it makes on them. Everyone you know and all the people you meet have the potential to be someone important in the lives of others. All they need is encouragement and motivation from you to help them reach their potential.

5. ANYBODY WHO HELPS SOMEBODY INFLUENCES A LOT OF BODIES

The final thing you need to understand about people is that when you help one person, you're really impacting a lot of other people. What you give to one person overflows into the lives of all the people that person impacts. The nature of influence is to multiply. It even impacts you because when you help others and your motives are good, you always receive more than you can ever give. Most people are so genuinely grateful when another person makes them feel special that they never tire of showing their gratitude.

CHOOSE TO UNDERSTAND OTHERS

In the end, the ability to understand people is a choice. It's true that some people are born with great instincts that enable them to understand how others think and feel. But even if you aren't instinctively a people person, you can improve your ability to work with others. Every person is capable of having the ability to understand, motivate, and ultimately influence others.

PART II

THE BUILDING BLOCKS OF RELATIONSHIPS

3

How Can I Encourage Others?

Believing in people before *they have proved themselves is the key to motivating people to reach their potential.*

Everyone loves encouragement. It lifts them up when they're down and motivates them when they're feeling discouraged. To be an encourager, you need to believe the best in people, to have faith in them. In fact, faith is essential for building and maintaining all positive relationships, yet it's a scarce commodity today. Take a look at the following four facts about faith:

1. Most People Don't Have Faith in Themselves

Not long ago I saw a *Shoe* comic strip by Jeff MacNelly that showed Shoe, the crusty newspaper editor, standing on the mound in a baseball game. His catcher says to him, "You've got to have faith in your curve ball." In the next frame Shoe remarks, "It's easy for him to say. When it comes to believing in myself, I'm an agnostic."

That's the way too many people feel today. They have

trouble believing in themselves. They believe they will fail. Even when they see a light at the end of the tunnel, they're convinced it's a train. They see a difficulty in every responsibility. But the reality is that difficulties seldom defeat people; lack of faith in themselves usually does it. With a little faith in themselves, people can do miraculous things. But without, they have a really tough time.

2. MOST PEOPLE DON'T HAVE SOMEONE WHO HAS FAITH IN THEM

In *Just for Today*, James Keller tells this story: "A sidewalk flower vendor was not doing any business. Suddenly a happy thought struck him and he put up this sign. 'This gardenia will make you feel important all day long for 10 cents.' All at once his sales began to increase."

In our society today, most people feel isolated. The strong sense of community that was once enjoyed by most Americans has become rare. And many people don't have the family support that was more common thirty or forty years ago. For example, evangelist Bill Glass noted, "Over 90 percent of prison inmates were told by parents while growing up, 'They're going to put you in jail.'" Instead of teaching their children to believe in themselves, some parents are tearing them down. For many people, even those who are closest to them don't believe in them. They have no one on their side. No wonder even a little thing like a flower can make a difference in how a person approaches the day.

3. Most People Can Tell When Someone Else Has Faith in Them

People's instincts are pretty good at knowing when others have faith in them. They can sense if your belief is genuine or phony. And truly having faith in someone can change his or her life.

In his book *Move Ahead with Possibility Thinking*, my friend Robert Schuller, pastor of the Crystal Cathedral in Garden Grove, California, tells a wonderful story about an incident that changed his life as a boy. It occurred when his uncle had faith in him and showed it in his words and actions:

> His car drove past the unpainted barn and stopped in a cloud of summer dust at our front gate. I ran bare-footed across the splintery porch and saw my uncle Henry bound out of the car. He was tall, very hand-some, and terribly alive with energy. After many years overseas in China, he was visiting our Iowa farm. He ran up to the old gate and put both of his big hands on my four-year-old shoulders. He smiled widely, ruffled my uncombed hair, and said, "Well! I guess you're

Robert! I think you are going to be a preacher some-day." That night I prayed secretly, "And dear God, make me a preacher when I grow up!" I believe that God made me a POSSIBILITY THINKER then and there.

Always remember that your goal is not to get people to think more highly of you. It's to get them to think more highly of themselves. Have faith in them, and they will begin to do exactly that.

4. Most People Will Do Anything to Live Up to Your Faith in Them

People rise or fall to meet your level of expectations for them. If you express skepticism and doubt in others, they will return your lack of confidence with mediocrity. But if you believe in them and expect them to do well, they will go the extra mile trying to do their best. And in the process, they and you benefit. John H. Spalding expressed the thought this way: "Those who believe in our ability do more than stimulate us. They create for us an atmosphere in which it becomes easier to succeed."

How to Become a Believer in People

I'm fortunate because I grew up in a positive, affirming envi-ronment. As a result, I have an easy time believing in people and expressing that belief. But I realize that not everyone had the benefit of a positive upbringing. Most people need to *learn* how to have faith in others. To build your belief in others, try using these suggestions, created using the initial letters of the word *BELIEVE.*

Believe in Them Before They Succeed

Everyone loves a winner. It's easy to have faith in people who have already proved themselves. It's much tougher to believe in people *before* they have proved themselves. But that is the key to motivating people to reach their potential. You have to believe in them first, before they become successful, and sometimes before you can persuade them to believe in themselves.

Some people in your life desperately want to believe in themselves but have little hope. As you interact with them, remember the motto of French World War I hero Marshal Ferdinand Foch: "There are no hopeless situations; there are only men and women who have grown hopeless about them." Every person has seeds of greatness within, even though they may currently be dormant. But when you believe in people, you water the seeds and give them the chance to grow.

Emphasize Their Strengths

Many people mistakenly think that to build relationships and be influential, they have to be an "authority" and point out others' deficiencies. People who try that approach become like Lucy from the comic strip *Peanuts* by Charles Schulz. In one strip Lucy told poor Charlie Brown, "You're in the shadow of your own goal posts! You are a miscue! You are three putts on the eighteenth green! You are a seven-ten split in the tenth frame. . . . You are a missed free throw, a shanked nine iron and a called third strike! Do you understand? Have I made myself clear?" That's hardly a way to positively impact the life of another person!

The road to building positive relationships lies in exactly the opposite direction. The best way to show people your faith in them and motivate them is to focus your attention on their strengths. According to author and advertising executive Bruce Barton, "Nothing splendid has ever been achieved except by those who dared believe that something inside them was superior to circumstances." By emphasizing people's strengths, you're helping them believe that they possess what they need to succeed.

BELIEVING IN PEOPLE BEFORE THEY HAVE PROVED THEMSELVES IS THE KEY TO MOTIVATING PEOPLE TO REACH THEIR POTENTIAL.

Praise them for what they do well, both privately and publicly. Tell them how much you appreciate their positive qualities and their skills. And anytime you have the opportunity to compliment and praise them in the presence of their family and close friends, do it.

LIST THEIR PAST SUCCESSES

Even when you emphasize people's strengths, they may need further encouragement to show them you believe in them and to get them motivated. Entrepreneur Mary Kay Ash, founder of Mary Kay cosmetics, advised, "Everyone has an invisible sign hanging from his neck saying, 'Make me feel important!' Never forget this message when working with people." One of the best ways to do that is to help people remember their past successes.

The account of David and Goliath presents a classic example of how past successes can help a person have faith in himself. You may remember the story from the Bible. A nine-foot-tall Philistine champion named Goliath stood before the army of Israel and taunted them every day for forty days, daring them to send out a warrior to face him. On the fortieth day a young shepherd named David came to the front lines to deliver food to his brothers, who were in Israel's army. While he was there, he witnessed the giant's contemptuous display of taunts and challenges. David was so infuriated that he told King Saul he wanted to face the giant in battle. Here's what happened next:

Saul replied, "You are not able to go out against this Philistine and fight him; you are only a boy, and he has been a fighting man from his youth." But David said to Saul, "Your servant has been keeping his father's sheep. When a lion or a bear came and carried off a sheep from the flock, I went after it, struck it and rescued the sheep from its mouth. When it turned on me, I seized it by its hair, struck it and killed it. Your servant has killed both the lion and the bear. . . . The LORD who delivered me from the paw of the lion and the paw of the bear will deliver me from the hand of this Philistine."[1]

David looked back on his past successes, and he had confidence in his future actions. And of course, when he faced the giant, he felled him like a tree, using nothing but a rock and sling. And when he cut off Goliath's head his success inspired his fellow countrymen; they routed the Philistine army.

Not everyone has the natural ability to recognize past successes and draw confidence from them. Some people need help. If you can show others that they have done well in the past and help them see that their past victories have paved the way for future success, they'll be better able to move into action. Listing past successes helps others believe in themselves.

Instill Confidence When They Fail

When you have encouraged people and put your faith in them, and they begin to believe they can succeed in life, they soon reach a critical crossroads. The first time or two that they fail—and they will fail because it's a part of life— they have two choices. They can give in or go on.

Some people are resilient and willing to keep trying in order to succeed, even when they don't see immediate progress. But others aren't that determined. Some will collapse at the first sign of trouble. To give them a push and inspire them, you need to keep showing your confidence in them, even when they're making mistakes or doing poorly.

One of the ways to do that is to tell about your past troubles and traumas. Sometimes people think that if you're currently successful, you have always been that way. They don't realize that you have had your share of flops, failures, and fumbles. Show them that success is a journey—a process, not a destination. When they realize that you have failed and yet still managed to succeed, they'll realize that it's okay to fail. And their confidence will remain intact. They will learn to think the way baseball legend Babe Ruth did when he said, "Never let the fear of striking out get in the way."

EXPERIENCE SOME WINS TOGETHER

It's not enough just knowing failure is a part of moving forward in life. To really become motivated to succeed, people need to believe they can win.

Winning is motivation. Novelist David Ambrose acknowledged this truth: "If you have the will to win, you have achieved half your success; if you don't, you have achieved half your failure." Coming alongside others to help them experience some wins with you gives them reasons to believe they will succeed. And in the process, they sense victory. That's when incredible things begin to happen in their lives.

To help people believe they can achieve victory, put them in a position to experience small successes. Encourage them to perform tasks or take on responsibilities you know that they can handle and do well. And give them the assistance they need to succeed. In time as their confidence grows, they will take on more difficult challenges, but they will be able to face them with confidence and competence because of the positive track record they're developing.

VISUALIZE THEIR FUTURE SUCCESS

An experiment performed with laboratory rats measured their motivation to live under different circumstances. Scientists dropped a rat into a jar of water that had been placed in total darkness, and they timed how long the animal would continue swimming before it gave up and allowed itself to drown. They found that the rat lasted little more than three minutes.

Then they dropped another rat into the same kind of jar, but instead of placing it in total darkness, they allowed a ray of light to shine into it. Under those circumstances, the rat kept swimming for thirty-six hours. That's more than seven hundred times longer than the one in the dark! Because the rat could see, it continued to have hope.

If that is true of laboratory animals, think of how strong the effect of visualization can be on people, who are capable of higher reasoning. It's been said that a person can live forty days without food, four days without water, four minutes without air, but only four seconds without hope. Each time you cast a vision for others and paint a picture of their future success, you build them up, motivate them, and give them reasons to keep going.

Expect a New Level of Living

German statesman Konrad Adenauer observed: "We all live under the same sky, but we don't all have the same horizon." Make it your goal to help others see beyond today and their current circumstances and dream big dreams. When you put your faith in people, you help them expand their horizons and motivate them to move to a whole new level of living.

Putting your faith in others involves taking a chance. But the rewards outweigh the risks. Robert Louis Stevenson said, "To be what we are, and to become what we are capable of becoming, is the only end of life." When you put your faith in others, you help them reach their potential. You become an important relationship in their lives—and they in yours.

4

How Can I Connect with People?

Always remember, the heart comes before the head.

I love communicating. It's one of my passions. Although I've spent more than thirty years speaking professionally, I'm always looking for ways to grow and keep improving in that area.

The Audience's Best Friend

No doubt you've heard of Elizabeth Dole. She is a lawyer by trade, was a cabinet member in the Reagan and Bush administrations, and was the president of the American Red Cross. She is a marvelous communicator. Her particular gift, which I witnessed in San Jose one day, was making me and everyone else in her audience feel as though she was really our friend. She made me glad I was there. The bottom line is that she really knows how to connect with people.

In 1996, she demonstrated that ability to the whole country when she spoke at the Republican National Convention.

If you watched it on television, you know what I'm talking about. When Elizabeth Dole walked out into the audience that night, they felt that she was their best friend. She was able to develop an amazing connection with them. I also felt that connection, even though I was sitting in my living room at home watching her on television. Once she finished her talk, I would have followed her anywhere.

BOB NEVER MADE THE CONNECTION

Also speaking at that convention was Bob Dole, Elizabeth's husband—not surprising since he was the Republican nominee for the presidential race. Anyone who watched would have observed a remarkable difference between the communication abilities of the two speakers. Where Elizabeth was warm and approachable, Bob appeared stern and distant. Throughout the campaign, he never seemed to be able to connect with the people.

Many factors come into play in the election of a president of the United States, but not least among them is the ability of a candidate to connect with his audience. A lot has been written about the Kennedy-Nixon debates of the 1960 election. One of the reasons John F. Kennedy succeeded was that he was able to make the television audience feel connected to him. The same kind of connection developed between Ronald Reagan and his audiences. And in the 1992 election, Bill Clinton worked extremely hard to develop a sense of connection with the American people—to do it he even appeared on the talk show *Arsenio* and played the saxophone.

> YOU CAN'T MOVE PEOPLE TO ACTION UNLESS YOU FIRST
> MOVE THEM WITH EMOTION. THE HEART COMES
> BEFORE THE HEAD.

I believe Bob Dole is a good man. But I also know he never connected with the people. Ironically, after the presidential race was over, he appeared on *Saturday Night Live,* a show that made fun of him during the entire campaign, implying that he was humorless and out of touch. On the show Dole came across as relaxed, approachable, and able to make fun of himself. And he was a hit with the audience. He had finally connected.

THE HEART COMES FIRST

You first have to touch people's hearts before you ask them for a hand. All great communicators recognize this truth and act on it almost instinctively. You can't move people to action unless you first move them with emotion. The heart comes before the head.

An outstanding orator and African-American leader of the nineteenth century was Frederick Douglass. It's said that he had a remarkable ability to connect with people and move their hearts when he spoke. Historian Lerone Bennett said of Douglass, "He could make people *laugh* at a slave owner preaching the duties of Christian obedience; could make them *see* the humiliation of a Black maiden ravished by a brutal slave owner; could make them *hear* the sobs of a mother separated from her child. Through him, people could cry, curse, and *feel*; through him they could *live* slavery."

CONNECT IN PUBLIC AND PRIVATE

Connecting with people isn't something that needs to happen only when communicating to groups of people. It needs to happen with individuals. And the stronger the relationship between individuals, the more beneficial it will be and the more likely the follower will want to help the leader. That is one of the most important principles I've taught my staff over the years. My staff used to groan every time I would say, "People don't care how much you know until they know how much you care," but they also knew that it was true. You develop credibility with people when you connect with them and show that you genuinely want to help them.

Connect with People One at a Time

A key to connecting with others is recognizing that even in a group, you have to relate to people as individuals. General Norman Schwarzkopf remarked, "I have seen competent leaders who stood in front of a platoon and all they saw was a platoon. But great leaders stand in front of a platoon and see it as 44 individuals, each of whom has aspirations, each of whom wants to live, each of whom wants to do good."[1] That's the only way to connect with people.

Put a "10" on Every Person's Head

One of the best things you can do for people is to expect the best of them. I call it putting a "10" on everyone's head. It helps others think more highly of themselves, and at the same time, it also helps you. According to Jacques Wiesel, "A survey of one hundred self-made millionaires showed only one common denominator. These highly successful men and women could only see the good in people."

Benjamin Disraeli understood and practiced this concept, and it was one of the secrets of his charisma. He once said, "The greatest good you can do for another is not just to share your riches but to reveal to him his own." If you appreciate others, encourage them, and help them reach their potential, they will connect with you.

THE TOUGHER THE CHALLENGE, THE GREATER THE CONNECTION

Never underestimate the power of building relationships with people. If you've ever studied the lives of notable military commanders, you have probably noticed that the best ones understood how to connect with people. I once read that during World War I in France, General Douglas MacArthur told a battalion commander before a daring charge, "Major, when the signal comes to go over the top, I want you to go first, before your men. If you do, they'll follow." Then MacArthur removed the Distinguished Service Cross from his uniform and pinned it on the major. He had, in effect, awarded him for heroism before asking him to exhibit it. And of course, the major led his men, they followed him over the top, and they achieved their objective.

THE RESULT OF CONNECTION IN THE WORKPLACE

When a leader has done the work to connect with his people, you can see it in the way the organization functions. Among employees there are incredible loyalty and a strong work ethic. The vision of the leader becomes the aspiration of the people. The impact is incredible.

You can also see the results in other ways. On Boss's Day in 1994, a full-page ad appeared in *USA Today*. It was contracted and paid for by the employees of Southwest Airlines, and it was addressed to Herb Kelleher, the company's CEO:

Thanks, Herb
For remembering every one of our names.
For supporting the Ronald McDonald House.
For helping load baggage on Thanksgiving.
For giving everyone a kiss (and we mean everyone).
For listening.
For running the only profitable major airline.
For singing at our holiday party.
For singing only once a year.
For letting us wear shorts and sneakers to work.
For golfing at The LUV Classic with only one club.
For outtalking Sam Donaldson.
For riding your Harley Davidson into Southwest
    Headquarters.
For being a friend, not just a boss.
Happy Boss's Day from Each One of Your 16,000
    Employees.[2]

A display of affection like that occurs only when a leader has worked hard to connect with his people.

Don't ever underestimate the importance of building relational bridges between yourself and others around you. There's an old saying: To lead yourself, use your head; to lead others, use your heart. Always touch a person's heart before you ask him for a hand.

5

How Can I Become
a Better Listener?

*Treat every person as if he or she were the
most important person in the world.*

Edgar Watson Howe once joked, "No man would listen to you talk if he didn't know it was his turn next." Unfortunately, that accurately describes the way too many people approach communication—they're too busy waiting for their turn to really listen to others. But successful people understand the incredible value of becoming a good listener.

The ability to skillfully listen is the foundation to building positive relationships with others. When Lyndon B. Johnson was a junior senator from Texas, he kept a sign on his office wall that read, "You ain't learnin' nothin' when you're doin' all the talkin'." And Woodrow Wilson, the twenty-eighth American president, once said, "The ear of the leader must ring with the voices of the people."

THE VALUE OF LISTENING

Consider these benefits to listening:

LISTENING SHOWS RESPECT

A mistake that people often make in communicating is trying very hard to impress the other person. They try to make themselves appear smart, witty, or entertaining. But if you want to relate well to others, you have to be willing to focus on what they have to offer. Be *impressed* and *interested*, not *impressive* and *interesting*. Poet-philosopher Ralph Waldo Emerson acknowledged, "Every man I meet is in some way my superior, and I can learn of him." Remember that and listen, and the lines of communication will really open up.

LISTENING BUILDS RELATIONSHIPS

Dale Carnegie, author of *How to Win Friends and Influence People*, advised, "You can make more friends in two weeks by becoming a good listener than you can in two years trying to get people interested in you." Carnegie was incredibly gifted at understanding relationships. He recognized that people who are self-focused and who talk about themselves and their concerns all the time rarely develop strong relationships with others. David Schwartz noted in *The Magic of Thinking Big*, "Big people monopolize the listening. Small people monopolize the talking."

By becoming a good listener, you are able to connect with others on more levels and develop stronger, deeper relationships because you are meeting a need. Author C. Neil Strait pointed out that "everyone needs someone who he feels really listens to him." When you become that important listener, you help that person.

Listening Increases Knowledge

Wilson Mizner said, "A good listener is not only popular everywhere, but after a while he knows something." It's amazing how much you can learn about your friends and family, your job, the organization you work in, and yourself when you decide to really listen to others. But not everyone clues into this benefit. For example, I once heard a story about a tennis pro who was giving a lesson to a new student. After watching the novice take several swings at the tennis ball, the pro stopped him and suggested ways he could improve his stroke. But each time he did, the student interrupted him, gave a different opinion of the problem, and stated how it should be solved. After several interruptions, the pro began to nod his head in agreement.

When the lesson ended, a woman who had been watching said to the pro, "Why did you go along with that arrogant man's stupid suggestions?"

The pro smiled and replied, "I learned a long time ago that

it is a waste of time to try to sell real *answers* to anyone who just wants to buy *echoes*."

Beware of putting yourself into a position where you think you know all the answers. Anytime you do, you'll be putting yourself in danger. It's almost impossible to think of yourself as "the expert" and continue growing and learning at the same time. All great learners are great listeners.

One common problem as people gain more authority is that they often listen to others less and less, especially the people who report to them. While it's true that the higher you go, the less you are required to listen to others, it's also true that your need for good listening skills increases. The farther you get from the front lines, the more you have to depend on others to get reliable information. Only if you develop good listening skills early, and then continue to use them, will you be able to gather the information you need to succeed.

As you proceed through life and become more successful, don't lose sight of your need to keep growing and improving yourself. And remember, a deaf ear is evidence of a closed mind.

LISTENING GENERATES IDEAS

Good companies have a reputation for listening to their people. Brinker International, owner of Chili's, On the

Border, Romano's Macaroni Grill, and other restaurant chains, is one of the nation's best-run food service chains according to *Restaurants and Institutions* magazine. Almost 80 percent of its restaurants' menu items have come from suggestions made by unit managers.

What's good for effective companies is good for individuals. When you consistently listen to others, you never suffer for ideas. People love to contribute, especially when their leader shares the credit with them. If you give people opportunities to share their thoughts, and you listen with an open mind, there will always be a flow of new ideas. And even if you hear ideas that won't work, just listening to them can often spark other creative thoughts in you and others. You'll never know how close you are to a million-dollar idea unless you're willing to listen.

Listening Builds Loyalty

A funny thing happens when you don't make a practice of listening to people. They find others who will. Anytime employees, spouses, colleagues, children, or friends no longer believe they are being listened to, they seek out people who will give them what they want. Sometimes the consequences can be disastrous: the end of a friendship, lack of authority at work, lessened parental influence, or the breakdown of a marriage.

On the other hand, practicing good listening skills draws people to you. Everyone loves a good listener and is attracted to him or her. And if you consistently listen to others, valuing them and what they have to offer, they are likely to develop a strong loyalty to you, even when your authority with them is unofficial or informal.

LISTENING IS A GREAT WAY TO HELP OTHERS AND YOURSELF

Roger G. Imhoff urged, "Let others confide in you. It may not help you, but it will surely help them." At first glance, listening to others may appear to benefit only them. But when you become a good listener, you put yourself in a position to help yourself too. You have the ability to develop strong relationships, gather valuable information, and increase your understanding of yourself and others.

HOW TO DEVELOP LISTENING SKILLS

To become a good listener, you have to want to hear. But you also need some skills to help you. Here are nine suggestions to help you become a better listener:

1. LOOK AT THE SPEAKER

The whole listening process begins with giving the other person your undivided attention. As you interact with someone, don't catch up on other work, shuffle papers, do the dishes, or watch television. Set aside the time to focus only on the other person. And if you don't have the time at that moment, then schedule it as soon as you can.

2. DON'T INTERRUPT

Most people react badly to being interrupted. It makes them feel disrespected. And according to Robert L. Montgomery, author of *Listening Made Easy*, "It's just as rude to step on other people's ideas as it is to step on their toes."

People who tend to interrupt others generally do so for one of these reasons:

- They don't place enough value on what the other person has to say.

- They want to impress others by showing how smart and intuitive they are.

- They're too excited by the conversation to let the other person finish talking.

If you are in the habit of interrupting other people, examine your motives and determine to make a change. Give people the time they need to express themselves. And don't feel that one of you has to speak all the time. Periods of silence can give you a chance to reflect on what's been said so that you can respond appropriately.

3. FOCUS ON UNDERSTANDING

Have you ever noticed how quickly most people forget the things they hear? Studies at institutions such as Michigan State, Ohio State, Florida State, and the University of Minnesota indicate that most people can recall only 50 percent of what they hear immediately after hearing it. And as the time passes, their ability to remember continues to drop. By the next day, their retention is usually down to 25 percent.

One way to combat that tendency is to aim for understanding rather than just remembering the facts. Lawyer, lecturer, and author Herb Cohen emphasized, "Effective listening requires more than hearing the words transmitted. It demands that you find meaning and understanding in what is being said. After all, meanings are not in words, but in people."

4. DETERMINE THE NEED AT THE MOMENT

A lot of men and women find themselves in conflict because they occasionally communicate at cross-purposes. They neglect to determine the need of the other person at the moment of interaction. Men usually want to fix any problems they discuss; their need is resolution. Women, on the other hand, are more likely to tell about a problem simply to share it; they neither request nor desire solutions. Anytime you can determine the current need of the people you're communicating with, you can put whatever they say into the appropriate context. And you will be better able to understand them.

IF YOU SHOW PEOPLE HOW MUCH YOU CARE AND ASK QUESTIONS IN A NONTHREATENING WAY, YOU'LL BE AMAZED BY HOW MUCH THEY'LL TELL YOU.

---

5. CHECK YOUR EMOTIONS

Most people carry around emotional baggage that causes them to react to certain people or situations. Sigmund Freud states, "A man with a toothache cannot be in love," meaning that the toothache doesn't allow him to notice anything other than his pain. Similarly, anytime a person has an ax to grind, the words of others are drowned out by the sound of the grindstone.

Anytime that you become highly emotional when listening to another person, check your emotions—especially if your reaction seems to be stronger than the situation warrants. You don't want to make an unsuspecting person the recipient of your venting. Besides, even if your reactions are not due to an event from your past, you should always allow others to finish explaining their points of view, ideas, or convictions before offering your own.

6. SUSPEND YOUR JUDGMENT

Have you ever begun listening to another person tell a story and started to respond to it before he or she was finished? Just about everyone has. But the truth is that you can't jump to conclusions and be a good listener at the same time. As you talk to others, wait to hear the whole story before you respond. If you don't, you may miss the most important thing they intend to say.

7. SUM UP AT MAJOR INTERVALS

Experts agree that listening is most effective when it's active. John H. Melchinger suggests, "Comment on what you hear, and individualize your comments. For example, you can say, 'Cheryl, that's obviously very important to you.' It will help keep you on track as a listener. Get beyond, 'That's interesting.' If you train yourself to comment meaningfully, the speaker will know you are listening and may offer further information."

A technique for active listening is to sum up what the other person says at major intervals. As the speaker finishes one subject, paraphrase his or her main points or ideas before going on to the next one, and verify that you have gotten the right message. Doing that reassures the person and helps you stay focused on what he or she is trying to communicate.

8. Ask Questions for Clarity

Have you ever noticed that top reporters are excellent listeners? Take someone like Barbara Walters, for example. She looks at the speaker, focuses on understanding, suspends judgment, and sums up what the person has to say. People trust her and seem to be willing to tell her just about anything. But she practices another skill that helps her to gather more information and increase her understanding of the person she is interviewing. She asks good questions.

If you want to become an effective listener, become a good reporter—not a stick-the-microphone-in-your-face-and-bark-questions-at-you reporter, but someone who gently asks follow-up questions and seeks clarification. If you show people how much you care and ask in a nonthreatening way, you'll be amazed by how much they'll tell you.

9. Always Make Listening Your Priority

The last thing to remember when developing your listening skills is to make listening a priority, no matter how busy you become or how far you rise in your organization. A remarkable example of a busy executive who made time for listening was the late Sam Walton, founder of Wal-Mart and one of the richest men in America. He believed in listening to what people had to say, especially his employees. He once flew his plane to Mt. Pleasant, Texas, landed, and gave instructions to his copilot to meet him about one hundred miles down the road. He then rode in a Wal-Mart truck just so that he could chat with the driver. We should all give listening that kind of priority.

Many people take for granted the ability to listen. Most people consider listening to be easy, and they view themselves as pretty good listeners. But while it's true that most people are able to hear, fewer are capable of really listening. However, it's never too late to become a good listener. It can change your life—and the lives of the people in your life.

PART III

THE GROWTH
OF RELATIONSHIPS

How Can I Build
Trust with Others?

*When your words and actions match,
people know they can trust you.*

In his best-selling book *The Seven Habits of Highly Effective People,* Stephen Covey wrote about the importance of integrity to a person's success:

> If I try to use human influence strategies and tactics of how to get other people to do what I want, to work better, to be more motivated, to like me and each other—while my character is fundamentally flawed, marked by duplicity or insincerity—then, in the long run, I cannot be successful. My duplicity will breed distrust, and everything I do—even using so-called good human relations techniques—will be perceived as manipulative.
>
> It simply makes no difference how good the rhetoric is or even how good the intentions are; if there is little or no

trust, there is no foundation or permanent success. Only basic goodness gives life to technique.[1]

Integrity is crucial for business and personal success. A joint study conducted by the UCLA Graduate School of Management and Korn/Ferry International of New York City surveyed 1,300 senior executives. Seventy-one percent of them said that integrity was the quality most needed to succeed in business. And a study by the Center for Creative Research discovered that though many errors and obstacles can be overcome by a person who wants to rise to the top of an organization, that person is almost never able to move up in the organization if he compromises his integrity by betraying a trust.

INTEGRITY IS ABOUT THE SMALL THINGS

Integrity is important to building relationships. And it is the foundation upon which many other qualities for success are built, such as respect, dignity, and trust. If the foundation of integrity is weak or fundamentally flawed, then success becomes impossible. As author and friend Cheryl Biehl points out, "One of the realities of life is that if you can't trust a person at all points, you can't truly trust him or her at any point." Even people who are able to hide their lack of integrity for a period of time will eventually experience failure, and their relationships will suffer.

It's crucial to maintain integrity by taking care of the little things. Many people misunderstand that. They think they can do whatever they want when it comes to the small things because they believe that as long as they don't have any major lapses, they're doing well. But ethical principles are not flexible. A little white lie is still a lie. Theft is theft—whether it's $1, $1,000, or $1 million. Integrity commits itself to character over personal gain, to people over things, to service over power, to principle over convenience, to the long view over the immediate.

Nineteenth-century clergyman Philips Brooks maintained, "Character is made in the small moments of our lives." Anytime you break a moral principle, you create a small crack in the foundation of your integrity. And when times get tough, it becomes harder to act with integrity, not easier. Character isn't created in a crisis; it only comes to light. Everything you have done in the past—and the things you have neglected to do—come to a head when you're under pressure.

Developing and maintaining integrity require constant attention. Josh Weston, former chairman and CEO of Automatic Data Processing, Inc., says, "I've always tried to live with the following simple rule: 'Don't do what you wouldn't feel comfortable reading about in the newspapers the next day.'" That's a good standard all of us should keep.

Integrity Is an Inside Job

One of the reasons many people struggle with integrity issues is that they tend to look outside themselves to explain any deficiencies in character. But the development of integrity is an inside job. Take a look at the following three truths about integrity that go against common thinking:

1. Integrity Is Not Determined by Circumstances

It's true that our upbringing and circumstances affect who we are, especially when we are young. But the older we get, the greater the number of choices we make—for good or bad. Two people can grow up in the same environment, even in the same household, and one will have integrity and the other won't. Your circumstances are as responsible for your character as a mirror is for your looks. Who you see only reflects who you are.

2. Integrity Is Not Based on Credentials

In ancient times, brick makers, engravers, and other artisans used a symbol to mark the things they created. The symbol that each one used was his "character." The value of the work was in proportion to the skill with which the object was made. And only if the quality of the work was high was the character esteemed. In other words, the quality of the person and his work gave value to his credentials. If the work was good, so was the character. If it was bad, then the character was viewed as poor.

The same is true for us today. Character comes from who we are. But some people would like to be judged not by who they are, but by the titles they have earned or the position they hold, regardless of the nature of their character. Their desire is to influence others by the weight of their credentials rather than the strength of their character. But credentials can never accomplish what character can. Look at some differences between the two:

CREDENTIALS	CHARACTER
Are transient	Is permanent
Turn the focus to rights	Keeps the focus on responsibilities
Add value to only one person	Adds value to many people
Look to past accomplishments	Builds a legacy for the future

Often evoke jealousy in others	Generates respect and integrity
Can only get you in the door	Keeps you there

No number of titles, degrees, offices, designations, awards, licenses, or other credentials can substitute for basic, honest integrity when it comes to the power of influencing others.

3. INTEGRITY IS NOT TO BE CONFUSED WITH REPUTATION

Certainly a good reputation is valuable. King Solomon of ancient Israel stated, "A good name is more desirable than great riches."[2] But a good reputation exists because it is a reflection of a person's character. If a good reputation is like gold, then having integrity is like owning the mine. Worry less about what others think, and give your attention to your inner character. D. L. Moody wrote, "If I take care of my character, my reputation will take care of itself."

If you struggle with maintaining your integrity, and you're doing all the right things on the *outside*—but you're still getting the wrong results—something is wrong and still needs to be changed on the *inside*. Look at the questions on the following page. They may help you nail down areas that need attention.

Questions to Help You Measure Your Integrity

1. How well do I treat people if I gain nothing?

2. Am I transparent with others?

3. Do I role-play based on the person(s) I'm with?

4. Am I the same person in the spotlight as I am when I'm alone?

5. Do I quickly admit wrongdoing without being pressed to do so?

6. Do I put people ahead of my personal agenda?

7. Do I have an unchanging standard for moral decisions, or do circumstances determine my choices?

8. Do I make difficult decisions, even when they have a personal cost attached to them?

9. When I have something to say about people, do I talk *to* them or *about* them?

10. Am I accountable to at least one other person for what I think, say, and do?

Don't be too quick to respond to the questions. If character development is a serious area of need in your life, your tendency may be to skim through the questions, giving answers that describe how you wish you were rather than who you actually are. Take some time to reflect on each question, honestly considering it before answering. Then work on the areas where you're having the most trouble.

INTEGRITY IS YOUR BEST FRIEND

Integrity is your best friend. It will never betray you or put you in a compromising position. It keeps your priorities right. When you're tempted to take shortcuts, it helps you to stay the right course. When others criticize you unfairly, it helps you keep going and take the high road of not striking back. And when others' criticism is valid, integrity helps you to accept what they say, learn from it, and keep growing.

IF A GOOD REPUTATION IS LIKE GOLD, THEN HAVING
INTEGRITY IS LIKE OWNING THE MINE.

Abraham Lincoln once stated, "When I lay down the reins of this administration, I want to have one friend left. And that friend is inside myself." You could almost say that

Lincoln's integrity was his best friend while he was in office because he was criticized so viciously. Here is a description of what he faced as explained by Donald T. Phillips:

> Abraham Lincoln was slandered, libeled and hated perhaps more intensely than any man ever to run for the nation's highest office. . . . He was publicly called just about every name imaginable by the press of his day, including a grotesque baboon, a third-rate country lawyer who once split rails and now splits the Union, a coarse vulgar joker, a dictator, an ape, a buffoon, and others. The *Illinois State Register* labeled him "the craftiest and most dishonest politician that ever disgraced an office in America. . . ." Severe and unjust criticism did not subside after Lincoln took the oath of office, nor did it come only from Southern sympathizers. It came from within the Union itself, from Congress, from some factions within the Republican party, and initially, from within his own cabinet. As president, Lincoln learned that, no matter what he did, there were going to be people who would not be pleased.[3]

Through it all, Lincoln was a man of principle. And as Thomas Jefferson wisely said, "God grant that men of principle shall be our principal men."

INTEGRITY IS YOUR FRIENDS' BEST FRIEND

Integrity is your best friend. And it's also one of the best friends that your friends will ever have. When the people around you know that you're a person of integrity, they know that you want to influence them because of the opportunity to add value to their lives. They don't have to worry about your motives.

If you're a basketball fan, you probably remember Red Auerbach. He was the president and general manager of the Boston Celtics from 1967 to 1987. He truly understood how integrity adds value to others, especially when people are working together on a team. And he had a method of recruiting that was different from that of most NBA team leaders. When he reviewed a prospective player for the Celtics, his primary concern was the young man's character. While others focused almost entirely on statistics and individual performance, Auerbach wanted to know about a player's attitude. He figured that the way to win was to find players who would give their best work for the benefit of the team. A player who had outstanding ability but whose character was weak or whose desire was to promote only himself was not really an asset.

It has been said that you don't really know people until you have observed them when they interact with a child, when the car has a flat tire, when the boss is away, and when they think no one will ever know. But people with integrity never have to worry about that. No matter where they are, who they are with, or what kind of situation they find themselves in, they are consistent and live by their principles.

BECOME A PERSON OF INTEGRITY

In the end, you can bend your actions to conform to your principles, or you can bend your principles to conform to your actions. It's a choice you have to make. If you want to be successful, then you better choose the path of integrity because all other roads ultimately lead to ruin.

To become a person of integrity, you need to go back to the fundamentals. You may have to make some tough choices, but they'll be worth it.

COMMIT YOURSELF TO HONESTY, RELIABILITY, AND CONFIDENTIALITY

Integrity begins with a specific, conscious decision. If you wait until a moment of crisis before settling your integrity issues, you set yourself up to fail. Choose today to live by a strict moral code, and determine to stick with it no matter what happens.

DECIDE AHEAD OF TIME THAT YOU DON'T HAVE A PRICE

President George Washington perceived that "few men have the virtue to withstand the highest bidder." Some people can be bought because they haven't settled the money issue before the moment of temptation. The best way to guard yourself against a breach in integrity is to make a decision today that you won't sell your integrity: not for power, revenge, pride, or money—any amount of money.

EACH DAY, DO WHAT YOU SHOULD DO BEFORE WHAT YOU WANT TO DO

A big part of integrity is following through consistently on your responsibilities. Our friend Zig Ziglar says, "When you do the things you have to do when you have to do them, the day will come when you can do the things you want to do when you want to do them." Psychologist-philosopher William James stated the idea more strongly: "Everybody ought to do at least two things each day that he hates to do, just for the practice."

With integrity, you can experience freedom. Not only are you less likely to be enslaved by the stress that comes from bad choices, debt, deceptiveness, and other negative character issues, but you are free to influence others and add value to them in an incredible way. And your integrity opens the door for you to experience continued success.

If you know what you stand for and act accordingly, people can trust you. You are a model of the character and consistency that other people admire and want to emulate. And you've laid a good foundation, one that makes it possible for you to build positive relationships.

WHAT IS MY MOST
IMPORTANT RELATIONSHIP?

Succeed at home, and all other relationships become easier.

Did you know that according to the Bureau of Labor Statistics, families dissolve at a greater rate in the United States than in any other major industrialized country? And we also lead in the number of fathers absent from the home. U.S. divorce laws are the most permissible in the world, and people are using them at an alarming rate.[1] To some people, marriages and families have become acceptable casualties in the pursuit of success.

But many people are now realizing that the hope of happiness at the expense of breaking up a family is an illusion. You can't give up your marriage or neglect your children and gain true success. Building and maintaining strong families benefit us in every way, including in helping us become successful. Family life expert Nick Stinnet asserted more than a decade ago, "When you have a strong family life, you receive the message that you are loved, cared for and important. *The positive intake of love, affection, and respect . . . gives you inner resources to deal with life more successfully"* (emphasis added).

WORKING TO STAY TOGETHER

Fairly early in our marriage, Margaret and I realized that in my career, I would often have the opportunity to travel. And we decided that any time I got the chance to go someplace interesting or to attend an event that we knew would be exciting, she would come along with me, even when it was difficult financially. We've done a pretty good job of following through on that commitment over the years.

Margaret and I, with our kids Elizabeth and Joel Porter, have been to the capitals of Europe, the jungles of South America, the teeming cities of Korea, the rugged outback of Australia, and on safari in South Africa. We've met wonderful people of every race and a multitude of nationalities. We've had the chance to see and do things that will remain in our memories for the rest of our lives. I decided early on, what would it profit me to gain the whole world and lose my family?

I know that I wouldn't have experienced any measure of success in life without Margaret. But my gratitude to her and the children doesn't come from what they've brought me. It comes from who they are to me. When I reach the end of my days, I don't want Margaret, Elizabeth, or Joel Porter to say that I was a good author, speaker, pastor, or leader. My desire is that the kids think I'm a good father and that Margaret thinks I'm a good husband. That's what matters most. It's the measure of true success.

STEPS TO BUILDING A STRONG FAMILY

Good marriages and strong families are joys, but they don't just happen on their own. Dr. R. C. Adams, who studied thousands of marriages over a ten-year period, found that only 17 percent of the unions he studied could be considered truly happy. And Jarle Brors, former director of the Institute of Marriage and Family Relations in Washington, D.C., said, "We are finally realizing that we have to go back to the basics in order to reestablish the type of families that give us the type of security that children can grow up in." If we want to have solid families and healthy marriages, we have to work hard to create them.

If you have a family—or you intend to have one in the future—take a look at the following guidelines. They have helped to develop the Maxwell family, and I believe they can help you to strengthen yours.

EXPRESS APPRECIATION FOR EACH OTHER

I once heard someone joke that home is the place where family members go when they are tired of being nice to other people. Unfortunately, some homes seem to work that way. A salesman spends his day treating his clients with the utmost kindness, often in the face of rejection, in order to build his business, but he is rude to his wife when he comes home. Or a doctor spends the day being caring and compassionate with her patients, but she comes home exhausted and blows up with her children.

To build a strong family, you have to make your home a supportive environment. Psychologist William James observed, "In every person from the cradle to the grave, there is a deep craving to be appreciated." Feeling appreciated brings out the best in people. And when that appreciation comes in the home and is coupled with acceptance, love, and encouragement, the bonds between family members grow, and the home becomes a safe haven for everyone.

WHAT WOULD IT PROFIT ME TO GAIN THE
WHOLE WORLD AND LOSE MY FAMILY?

I've heard that for every negative remark to a family member, it takes four positive statements to counteract the damage. That's why it's so important to focus on the positive aspects of each other's personality and express unconditional love for each other, both verbally and nonverbally. Then the home becomes a positive environment for everyone.

STRUCTURE YOUR LIVES TO SPEND TIME TOGETHER

It's been said that the American home has become a domestic cloverleaf upon which family members pass each other while en route to a multitude of places and activities. That seems to be true. When I was a kid, I spent a lot of time with my parents, brother, and sister. We went on family vacations, usually in the car. As a parent, it's been harder for me to keep that tradition alive. We've been good about planning and taking vacations together, but sometimes we've had to be creative to have time together. For example, when the children were younger, I always tried to drive them to school in the morning to spend some time with them. But with all the things going on in our busy lives, we found that the only way to get time together was to plan it carefully.

Every month, I spend several hours examining my travel schedule, figuring out what lessons I need to write, thinking about the projects I have to complete, and so on. And at that time, I'll plan my work for the whole month. But before I mark any dates for work, I write in all the important dates for family activities. I'll block out time for birthdays, anniversaries, ball games, theater performances, graduation ceremonies, concerts, and romantic dinners. And I'll also schedule special one-on-one time with Margaret and each of the kids so that we can continue to build our relationships. Then once those are set, I'll plan my work schedule around them. I've done this for years, and it's been the only thing that's prevented my work from squeezing my family out of the schedule. I've found that if I don't strategically structure my life to spend time with my family, it won't happen.

DEAL WITH CRISIS IN A POSITIVE WAY

Every family experiences problems, but not all families respond to them in the same way. And that often separates a family that's close from one that's barely holding together. I've noticed that some people pursuing success seem to avoid the home environment. I suspect that one reason is that they are not able to handle family crisis situations well. They find it easier to try to avoid the problems altogether. But that's not a solution.

M. Scott Peck, author of *The Road Less Traveled,* has offered some remarkable insights on the subject of problems and how we handle them:

> It is in this whole process of meeting and solving problems that life has meaning. Problems are the cutting edge that distinguishes between success and failure. Problems call forth our courage and wisdom; indeed they create our courage and our wisdom. It is only because of problems that we grow mentally and spiritually. . . . It is through the pain of confronting

and resolving problems that we learn. As Benjamin Franklin said, "Those things that hurt, instruct."

If we are to grow as families and be successful at home as well as in the other areas of our lives, we must learn to cope with the difficulties we find there. Here are some strategies to help you with the problem-solving process:

- *Attack the problem, never the person.* Always try to be supportive of each other. Remember, you're all on the same side. So don't take your frustrations out on people. Instead, attack the problem.

- *Get all the facts.* Nothing can cause more damage than jumping to false conclusions during a crisis. Don't waste your emotional or physical energy chasing down a wrong problem. Before you try to find solutions, be sure you know what's really going on.

- *List all the options.* This may sound a bit analytical, but it really helps because you can look at emotional subjects with some objectivity. Besides, if you had a problem at work, you would probably be willing to go through this process. Give any family problem at least as much time and energy as you would a professional one.

- *Choose the best solution.* As you decide on a solution, always remember that people are your priority. Make your choices accordingly.

- *Look for the positives in the problem.* As Dr. Peck said, the tough things give us a chance to grow. No matter how bad things look at the moment, just about everything has something positive that comes from it.

- *Never withhold love.* No matter how bad things get or how angry you are, never withhold your love from your spouse or children. Sure, tell them how you feel. Acknowledge the problems. But continue loving family members unconditionally through it all.

This last point is the most important of all. When you feel loved and supported by your family, you can weather nearly any crisis. And you can truly enjoy success.

COMMUNICATE CONTINUALLY

An article in the *Dallas Morning News* reported that the average couple married ten years or more spends only thirty-seven minutes a week in meaningful communication. I could hardly believe it. Compare that to the fact that the average American spends almost five times longer than that watching television every day! No wonder so many marriages are in trouble. Just like anything else, good communication doesn't develop by itself. It must be developed, and that process takes time and effort. Here are some suggestions for helping you do exactly that:

- *Develop platforms for communication.* Be creative about finding reasons to talk to each other. Take walks together as a family where you can talk. Call your spouse a couple of times during the day. Meet for lunch one day a week. Offer to drive the kids to soccer practice so you can talk. Communication can happen almost anywhere.

- *Control communication killers.* The television and the telephone probably steal the most family communication time. Restrict the amount of time you give them, and you'd be amazed by how much time you have to talk.

- *Encourage honesty and transparency in conversations.* Differences of opinion are healthy and normal in a family. Encourage all family members to speak their minds, and then when they do, never criticize or ridicule them.

- *Adopt a positive communication style.* Be conscious of the way you interact with your family members. You may have adopted a style that stifles open communication. If you're in the habit of using any communication style other than a cooperative one, begin working immediately to change. You'll have to do that if you want to build your relationship with your family.

SHARE THE SAME VALUES

Today, families don't give values the same priority or attention as they once did. Boston College education professor William Kilpatrick said, "There is a myth that parents don't have the right to instill their values in their children. Once again, the standard dogma here is that children must create their own values. But of course, children have precious little chance to do that. . . . Does it make sense for parents to remain neutral bystanders when everyone else from script writers, to entertainers, to advertisers, to sex educators insist on selling their values to children?"[2]

Common values strengthen a family and are especially beneficial to children as they grow up. A study conducted by the Search Institute showed that in single-parent homes, children whose parent expresses and enforces standards thrive at twice the rate of children who don't have values promoted in a similar way.[3] And that doesn't even take into account whether the values are what we would consider positive.

The best way to get started in working toward sharing common values in your family is to identify the values you want to instill. If you're like most families, you've never done that before. But to be able to live them out, you first have to find them out. They are the three to seven things you're willing to go to the mat for.

Let me list for you the five we've identified in the Maxwell family so that you have an idea of what I'm talking about:

1. Commitment to God

2. Commitment to personal and family growth

3. Commonly shared experiences

4. Confidence in ourselves and others

5. The desire to make a contribution in life

The values you choose will undoubtedly be different from ours, but you need to identify them. If you've never done it before, set aside some time to talk about your values with your spouse and children. If your kids are older, include them in the process of identifying the values. Make it a discussion time. And never be reluctant to take on the role of model and teacher of your family's values. If you don't do it, someone else will.

BUILD YOUR MARRIAGE

Finally, if you are married, the best thing you can do to strengthen your family is to build your marriage relationship. It's certainly the best thing you can do for your spouse, but it also has an incredibly positive impact on your children. My friend Josh McDowell wisely stated, "The greatest thing a father can do for his children is to love their mother." And the greatest thing a mother can do for her children is to love their father.

A common missing ingredient in many marriages is dedication to make things work. Marriages may start because of love, but they finish because of commitment. Sexuality researcher Dr. Alfred Kinsey, who studied six thousand marriages and three thousand divorces, revealed that "there may be nothing more important in a marriage than a determination that it shall persist. With such a determination, individuals force themselves to adjust and to accept situations which would seem sufficient grounds for a breakup, if continuation of the marriage were not the prime objective." If you want to help your spouse, your children, and yourself, then become committed to building and sustaining a strong marriage.

NBA coach Pat Riley said, "Sustain a family life for a long period of time and you can sustain success for a long period of time. First things first. If your life is in order you can do whatever you want." There is definitely a correlation between family success and personal success. Not only does building strong family relationships lay the groundwork for future success, but it also gives life deeper meaning.

I believe that few people have ever been truly successful without a positive, supportive family. No matter how great people's accomplishments are, I think they're still missing something when they're working without the benefit of those close relationships. True, some people are called to be single, but they are rare. For most people, a good family helps you know your purpose and develop your potential, and it helps you enjoy the journey along the way with an intensity that isn't possible otherwise. And when it comes to sowing seeds that benefit others, who could possibly derive greater benefit from you than your own family members?

HOW CAN I SERVE AND LEAD PEOPLE AT THE SAME TIME?

You've got to love your people more than your position.

U.S. Army General H. Norman Schwarzkopf displayed highly successful leadership abilities in commanding the allied troops in the Persian Gulf War, just as he had done throughout his career, beginning in his days at West Point.

In Vietnam he turned around a battalion that was in shambles. The First Battalion of the Sixth Infantry—known as the "worst of the sixth"—went from laughingstock to effective fighting force and were selected to perform a more difficult mission. That turned out to be an assignment to what Schwarzkopf described as "a horrible, malignant place" called the Batangan Peninsula. The area had been fought over for thirty years, was covered with mines and booby traps, and was the site of numerous weekly casualties from those devices.

Schwarzkopf made the best of a bad situation. He introduced procedures to greatly reduce casualties, and whenever a soldier *was* injured by a mine, he flew out to check on the man, had him evacuated using his chopper, and talked to the other soldiers to boost their morale.

On May 28, 1970, a man was injured by a mine, and Schwarzkopf, then a colonel, flew to the man's location. While the helicopter was evacuating the injured soldier, another soldier stepped on a mine, severely injuring his leg. The man thrashed around on the ground, screaming and wailing. That's when everyone realized the first mine hadn't been a lone booby trap. They were all standing in the middle of a minefield.

Schwarzkopf believed the injured man could survive and even keep his leg—but only if he stopped flailing around. There was only one thing he could do. He had to go after the man and immobilize him. Schwarzkopf wrote,

> I started through the minefield, one slow step at a time, staring at the ground, looking for telltale bumps or little prongs sticking up from the dirt. My knees were shaking so hard that each time I took a step, I had to grab my leg and steady it with both hands before I could take another . . . It seemed like a thousand years before I reached the kid.

The 240-pound Schwarzkopf, who had been a wrestler at West Point, then pinned the wounded man and calmed him down. It saved his life. And with the help of an engineer team, Schwarzkopf got him and the others out of the minefield.

The quality that Schwarzkopf displayed that day could be described as heroism, courage, or even foolhardiness. But I think the word that best describes it is *servanthood*. On that day in May, the only way he could be effective as a leader was to serve the soldier who was in trouble.

Having a Servant's Heart

When you think of servanthood, do you envision it as an activity performed by relatively low-skilled people at the bottom of the positional totem pole? If you do, you have a wrong impression. Servanthood is not about position or skill. It's about attitude. You have undoubtedly met people in service positions who have poor attitudes toward servanthood: the rude worker at the government agency, the waiter who can't be bothered with taking your order, the store clerk who talks on the phone with a friend instead of helping you.

Just as you can sense when a worker doesn't want to help people, you can just as easily detect whether someone has a servant's heart. And the truth is that the best leaders desire to serve others, not themselves.

What does it mean to embody the quality of servanthood? A true servant leader:

1. Puts Others Ahead of His Own Agenda

The first mark of servanthood is the ability to put others ahead of yourself and your personal desires. It is more than being willing to put your agenda on hold. It means intentionally being aware of other people's needs, available to help them, and able to accept their desires as important.

2. Possesses the Confidence to Serve

The real heart of servanthood is security. Show me someone who thinks he is too important to serve, and I'll show you someone who is basically insecure. How we treat others is really a reflection of how we think about ourselves. Philosopher-poet Eric Hoffer captured that thought:

> The remarkable thing is that we really love our neighbor as ourselves; we do unto others as we do unto ourselves. We hate others when we hate ourselves. We are tolerant toward others when we tolerate ourselves. We forgive others when we forgive ourselves. It is not love of self but hatred of self which is at the root of the troubles that afflict our world.

Only secure leaders give power to others. It's also true that only secure people exhibit servanthood.

3. Initiates Service to Others

Just about anyone will serve if compelled to do so. And some will serve in a crisis. But you can really see the heart of someone who initiates service to others. Great leaders see the need, seize the opportunity, and serve without expecting anything in return.

4. Is Not Position-Conscious

Servant leaders don't focus on rank or position. When Colonel Norman Schwarzkopf stepped into that minefield, rank was the last thing on his mind. He was one person trying to help another. If anything, being the leader gave him a greater sense of obligation to serve.

5. Serves Out of Love

Servanthood is not motivated by manipulation or self-promotion. It is fueled by love. In the end, the extent of your influence and the quality of your relationships depend on the depth of your concern for others. That's why it's so important for leaders to be willing to serve.

How to Become a Servant

To improve your servanthood, do the following:

- *Perform small acts.* When was the last time you performed small acts of kindness for others? Start with those closest to you: your spouse, children, parents. Find ways today to do small things that show others you care.

- *Learn to walk slowly through the crowd.* I learned this great lesson from my father. I call it walking slowly through the crowd. The next time you attend a function with a number of clients, colleagues, or employees, make it your goal to connect with others by circulating among them and talking to people. Focus on each person you meet. Learn his name if you don't know it already. Make your agenda getting to know each person's needs, wants, and desires. Then later when you go home, make a note to yourself to do something beneficial for half a dozen of those people.

IT IS TRUE THAT THOSE WHO WOULD BE GREAT
MUST BE LIKE THE LEAST AND THE SERVANT OF ALL.

- *Move into action.* If an attitude of servanthood is conspicuously absent from your life, the best way to change it is to start serving. Begin serving with your body, and your heart will eventually catch up. Sign up to serve others for six months at your church, a community agency, or a volunteer organization. If your attitude still isn't good at the end of your term, do it again. Keep at it until your heart changes.

Where is your heart when it comes to serving others? Do you desire to become a leader for the perks and benefits? Or are you motivated by a desire to help others?

If you really want to become the kind of leader that people want to follow, you will have to settle the issue of servanthood. If your attitude is to be served rather than to serve, you may be headed for trouble. It is true that those who would be great must be like the least and the servant of all.

Albert Schweitzer wisely stated, "I don't know what your destiny will be, but one thing I know: The ones among you who will be really happy are those who have sought and found how to serve." If you want to be successful on the highest level, be willing to serve on the lowest. That's the best way to build relationships.

NOTES

Chapter 1
1. Michael K. Deaver, "The Ronald Reagan I Knew," *Parade*, 22 April 2001, 12.
2. Ibid., 10.
3. "Thirty Years with Reagan: A Chat with Author, Former Reagan Aide Michael Deaver," 20 April 2001 <www.abc-news.com>.
4. Ibid.

Chapter 2
1. Art Mortell, "How to Master the Inner Game of Selling," vol. 10, no. 7.
2. Ecclesiastes 4:9–12 NIV.

Chapter 3
1. 1 Samuel 17:33–37 NIV.

Chapter 4
1. H. Norman Schwarzkopf, "Lessons in Leadership," vol. 12, no. 5.

2. Kevin and Jackie Freiberg, *Nuts! Southwest Airlines' Crazy Recipe for Business* (New York: Broadway Books, 1996), 224.

Chapter 6
1. Stephen R. Covey, *The Seven Habits of Highly Effective People: Restoring the Character Ethic* (New York: Simon and Schuster, 1989).
2. Proverbs 22:1 NIV.
3. Donald T. Phillips, *Lincoln on Leadership: Executive Strategies for Tough Times* (New York: Warner Books, 1992), 66–67.

Chapter 7
1. Gary Bauer, "American Family Life," *Focus on the Family* magazine, July 1994, 2.
2. William Kirkpatrick, *Why Johnny Can't Tell Right from Wrong* (New York: Simon and Schuster, 1992).
3. Quoted in *Christianity Today*, 4 October 1993.

John Maxwell's REAL Leadership Series

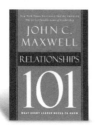

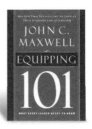

Relationships 101
ISBN 0-7852-6351-9

Equipping 101
ISBN 0-7852-6352-7

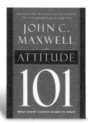

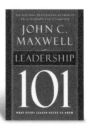

Attitude 101
ISBN 0-7852-6350-0

Leadership 101
ISBN 0-7852-6419-1

THOMAS NELSON
PUBLISHERS
Since 1798

Other Books by Dr. John C. Maxwell
Can Teach You How to Be a REAL Success

RELATIONSHIPS
Be a People Person (Victor Books)
Becoming a Person of Influence (Thomas Nelson)
The Power of Partnership in the Church (J. Countryman)
The Treasure of a Friend (J. Countryman)

EQUIPPING
The 17 Indisputable Laws of Teamwork (Thomas Nelson)
The 17 Essential Qualities of a Team Player (Thomas Nelson)
Developing the Leaders Around You (Thomas Nelson)
Partners in Prayer (Thomas Nelson)
Running with the Giants (Warner Books)
Success One Day at a Time (J. Countryman)
There's No Such Thing as Business Ethics (Warner Books)
Thinking for a Change (Warner Books)
Today Matters (Warner Books)

ATTITUDE
Be All You Can Be (Victor Books)
Failing Forward (Thomas Nelson)
The Power of Thinking (Honor Books)
Living at the Next Level (Thomas Nelson)
Think on These Things (Beacon Hill)
The Winning Attitude (Thomas Nelson)
Your Bridge to a Better Future (Thomas Nelson)
The Power of Attitude (Honor Books)

LEADERSHIP
The 21 Indispensable Qualities of a Leader (Thomas Nelson)
The 21 Irrefutable Laws of Leadership (Thomas Nelson)
The 21 Most Powerful Minutes in a Leader's Day (Thomas Nelson)
Developing the Leader Within You (Thomas Nelson)
Leadership Promises for Every Day (J. Countryman)
The Right to Lead (J. Countryman)
Your Road Map for Success (Thomas Nelson)

CONTINUE

We hope you've enjoyed *Relationships 101* and we want you to know tha
INJOY® we believe that building relationships is a key ingredient in leader
development. We are dedicated to developing you as a leader of excellen
and integrity by providing the finest resources and training for your pers
and professional growth.

YOUR Leadership Wired

Take the next step in developing the leadership potential in yourself and
those around you. We've made the first step as simple and as easy as poss
— it's FREE and it's delivered to your e-mail box twice a month!
Visit www.Relationships101book.com and sign up for *Leadership Wired* t

LEADERSHIP

Ready for a challenge that's a little meatier? We recommend
The 17 Indisputable Laws of Teamwork. Read the valuable
lessons within this book and you'll take the next giant step
toward becoming the leader you've always wanted to be.
Order online today at www.Relationships101book.com.

EDUCATION!

Visit **www.Relationships101book.com** and
sign up for your FREE subscription to
Leadership Wired today!

SHARE THESE

If you've found valuable insights within the pages of *Relationships 101,* why not share this treasure with friends, family, and business associates? Visit us at www.Relationships101book.com and order a copy for those you value!

LEADERSHIP

eat for holidays, anniversaries, and birthdays, let *Relationships 101* show those closest to you that you care about their personal and professional wth. Also, for you sales leaders, remember that *Relationships 101* makes great sales leave behind! Order today at www.Relationships101book.com.

LESSONS

Do you have children preparing to leave home for college, the military, or the business world? Give them a headstart on 1 incredible competitive advantage — building relationships! Visit us at www.Relationships101book.com and order them a copy of *Relationships 101* today.

WITH FRIENDS!

Order *Relationships 101* for a friend
at **www.Relationships101book.com**!

OTHER BOOKS BY JOHN C. MAXWELL

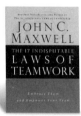

THE 17 INDISPUTABLE LAWS OF TEAMWORK

Everyone who works with people is realizing that the old autocratic method of leadership simply doesn't work. The way to win is to build a great team.

John C. Maxwell has been teaching the benefits of leadership and team building for years. Now he tackles the importance of teamwork head on, writing about teamwork being necessary for every kind of leader, and showing how team building can improve every area of your life.

ISBN 0-7852-7434-0

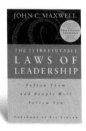

THE 21 IRREFUTABLE LAWS OF LEADERSHIP

What would happen if a top expert with more than thirty years of leadership experience were willing to distill everything he had learned about leadership into a handful of life-changing principles for you? It would change your life.

John C. Maxwell has done exactly that in *The 21 Irrefutable Laws of Leadership*. He has combined insights learned from his thirty-plus years of leadership successes and mistakes with observations from the worlds of business, politics, sports, religion, and military conflict. The result is a revealing study of leadership delivered as only a communicator like Maxwell can.

ISBN 0-7852-7431-6

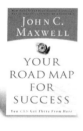

YOUR ROAD MAP FOR SUCCESS

Defining success is a difficult task. Most people equate it with wealth, power, and happiness. However, true success is not a thing you acquire or achieve. Rather, it is a journey you take your whole life long. In a refreshingly straightforward style, John Maxwell shares unique insights into what it means to be successful. And he reveals a definition that puts genuine success within your reach yet motivates you to keep striving for your dreams.

ISBN 0-7852-6596-1

THOMAS NELSON
PUBLISHERS
Since 1798

About the Author

John C. Maxwell, known as America's expert on leadership, speaks in person to hundreds of thousands of people each year. He has communicated his leadership principles to Fortune 500 companies, the United States Military Academy at West Point, and sports organizations such as the NCAA, the NBA, and the NFL.

Maxwell is the founder of several organizations, including Maximum Impact, dedicated to helping people reach their leadership potential. He is the author of more than thirty books, including *Developing the Leader Within You, Failing Forward, Your Road Map for Success, There's No Such Thing as Business Ethics*, and *The 21 Irrefutable Laws of Leadership*, which has sold more than one million copies.